Wildly Undone

Valerie Bruce

BookLeaf Publishing
India | USA | UK

Presentation by *BookLeaf Publishing*

Web: www.bookleafpub.com

E-mail: info@bookleafpub.com

ISBN:

First edition 2024

DEDICATION

For my children,

who always remind me that love and truth are loud, wild, patient, and worth everything.

ACKNOWLEDGEMENT

To my children, thank you for being the heartbeat of my life. Your light, strength, laughter, and beautiful minds are the reason I keep going. You teach me every day what it means to show up with love, even in the chaos.

To those who have stood beside me in the dark through the trauma, the healing, the unraveling, and the rebuilding, thank you! Your presence, your patience, and your quiet understanding have carried me when I couldn't carry myself.

To the readers holding this book: thank you for giving my words a home. If these pages speak to even one part of your story, I'm honored. You are not alone.

And finally, to the version of me who picked up the pen when everything felt like too much, I'm proud of you. For telling the truth. For staying. For turning pain into poetry.

I may be wildly undone, but I am still here.
And that is everything.

PREFACE

Wildly Undone isn't polished. It's not perfect. It's not tied in pretty bows, and that's exactly the point. These pages were written in the thick of it: through grief, motherhood, trauma, the unraveling of friendships, and the weight of being misunderstood by people who only ever knew the version of me that smiled through whatever was going on.

This is for the version of me who fought and is still fighting to stand on solid ground.

I'm a mother of two brilliant, neurodivergent children who teach me daily about resilience, imagination, and what it means to feel everything fully. I'm also a woman learning to hold herself with grace after being broken in ways that rarely leave visible scars. Writing became my release valve, the only way I knew to survive when I couldn't make sense of the storm out loud.

This collection is messy. Tender. Unfiltered. Real.

I wrestled with which poems to share, afraid of how they'd be misread, afraid of what people might say. I edited, second-guessed, deleted, and rewrote. And then one night, I stopped. I wrote from the gut. From the places that burned. From silence, anger, heartbreak, and hard truths I needed to finally speak.

Wildly Undone is for anyone who has ever felt like too much or not enough. For those brought to their knees and somehow still found the strength to rise again, even if the rising was slow, even if it still hurt.

My hope is that somewhere in these pages, you feel less alone. That you see pieces of yourself here. That even in your most unraveling moments, you remember you are wildly worthy of love, of rest, and of peace.

Thank you for being here.

Val

Let It

I opened my eyes and for the first time
I really looked.
Not for answers, not for signs, not for something
to blame or to fix
but just…to see.

The world didn't apologize for the mess.
It just was.
A mosaic of joy and jagged edges, a heartbreak
held together with dandelion wishes and duct
tape.

And suddenly,
I didn't need it to be perfect.
I didn't need me to be perfect.

I saw the flowers the ones that bloom with no
one watching, the ones that grow through
sidewalk cracks, whispering,
"Even here, life happens."

I saw the trees bent and bruised by wind, still
dancing.
Still reaching for a sun that sometimes forgets to
shine.

I heard the birds not in harmony, but in honest chaos, each one screaming its own name into the wide blue sky like it mattered. Because it does.

I saw the storms too the ones that rattle windowpanes and hearts.
And I didn't flinch.
Because I've been the thunder.
I've been the lightning.
I've been the wreckage left behind.
And I'm still here.

So I let go of the version of me that always had to hold it all,
that whispered, "Be good" when I really wanted to scream,
that begged, "Be brave," when I just needed to rest.

I let go of timelines,
checklists, and the illusion of control. Let go of "what if," and "almost," and "someday."

And I fell
not apart, but into the moment. Into the color and the chaos, the beauty and the lack. Because even emptiness has something to teach me.

So if you ask me what I've learned
I'll say this:
Let it all in.
Let it all go.
Let it hurt.
Let it heal.
Let it be loud.
Let it be still.
Let it surprise you.
Let it wreck you.
Let it remake you.

More Than Blood

You were never just my aunt.
That word,
it barely holds the weight of who you are.
You've always been more of a second heart, a steady voice, a kind of mother that love chose for me.

Not instead of, but alongside.
A different kind of sacred.
A different kind of strong.

You didn't raise me, but you raised me in every moment you saw me fully, every time you listened without rushing to fix, every truth you gave even when it stung.

You never let me feel like a guest in your heart.
You made space for my whole self
my softness, my rage, my mess, my dreams.

You've loved me in a way that never felt like "extra." Never "when you could." Just always. Just real.

And when I feel lost, when I'm spinning in fear or buried in doubt, I feel you quiet and steady like a hand on my back even when you're far away.

Because you were never just arms to run to. You were the voice that taught me how to run toward myself.
How to stand.
How to breathe.
How to cry without shame.

You are not the mother I was born to but the one who mothered me in moments I didn't know I needed it.
And I will always be your girl.
Not "the daughter you never had," but your daughter in all the ways that count.

You've held my pain without judgment. You've celebrated my joy like it was your own. You've been my mirror, my anchor, my truth-teller when sugarcoating would've been easier.

And you are a beautiful, bold soul, the kind of woman I pray the world never wears down. The kind of woman I am unspeakably lucky to call mine.

So here it is, plainly: I love you in ways I can't always say out loud.
And more than you will ever know, I carry your love as proof that family
can be chosen, can be magic, can be everything when we need it most.

I'm Not the Villain

I've lit fires
I swore I wouldn't strike
been both victim
and arsonist alike.

Spoke truths that cracked
broke myself open too
held my own smoke,
then let it settle on you.

No saint here
I've stung and scarred
but if you feel the burn,
look in the mirror hard.

I'm not the villain.
But I could be.
and just know
I'd own the part.

The Traitors in the Library with Wine & Provisions

They called it a sanctuary.
A little nook of dusty spines and secrets, where the wine was following, and so was the honesty, the laughter had weight, the kind that rattles the ribs and settles warm in the bones.

Three of us.
Women worn thin, laughing through the fray of school drop-offs, laundry mountains, and husbands who couldn't find the ketchup in the fridge they opened five times.

We swapped tales of forgetfulness, loneliness, the kind that makes you feel invisible in plain sight.
Of men who tried but needed instructions for empathy like they did for IKEA shelves.

You remember, don't you?
We spoke in sighs and eye rolls, found sisterhood in the daily grind.
And when I whispered, "I think I'm done, not angry, not broken, just…done," you reached for the wine, poured it like it was holy, and said

"You've carried enough," "Whatever you need we got you."

But when I left
when I stopped choosing the weight that didn't fit anymore
you disappeared.

No call.
No glass held out.
No porch light left on.

Instead, you huddled in group chats where I became the uncomfortable topic, rewritten as reckless, selfish, a disruption to your dinner routines.

Your husbands didn't stray
but you feared they'd think twice if you stood too close to me.
So, you tucked yourselves behind them, like shadows, like safety.

I became the warning, when I had only ever been the friend who said,
"You're not crazy. You're just tired." The one who listened when you needed to scream into a pillow about his snoring and his socks and the way he never really heard you.

But somehow, choosing peace for myself was choosing exile.

So here's to you two
the traitors in the library with wine and provisions.
You knew my heart.
You held my hurt. You passed me the corkscrew and the courage and then ran and hid.

I walked out, not because I wanted to be alone, but because I needed to be whole. You knew more than the cover story, you knew the depths that landed me in somewhere you never thought I'd go, and still you chose silence and misguided pride.

And now,
I drink to freedom.
To the truth.
To my own damn provisions.

May your silence keep you company.

Far From Gray

There's a spark in his laughter, a thunderous joy,
A wildfire heart in a blue-eyed boy.
His smile? A sunrise, brighter than gold,
He's five parts mischief, and stories untold.

They say his name may whisper Gray,
But oh he is color in the loudest way.
Crayon-box soul, neon dreams in his head,
He paints the world louder than anything said.

He's strong in the way that mountains admire,
With courage that glows like a campfire.
A punchline prince, a giggling king,
He turns the ordinary into everything.

Smarter than he'll ever believe or see,
He solves life's puzzles like they're meant to be.
And I? I breathe in rhythm with his pace, My
heartbeat syncs to his smiling face.

He is joy in motion, my reason, my light
A burst of color in the darkest night.
So say his name, but don't mistake
This boy is far from gray, in every way.

Do You Know the Way Out?

You are a haunting I welcomed. You moved in with no intention of staying, but left your scent on every memory like smoke in old clothes.

And maybe I don’t want to forget. Maybe I just want to wonder if you ever feel lost and look for my name in the spaces between now and then.

But you were always better at leaving. And I was always better at standing still.

So here I am again in a hallway full of frames with our half-finished paintings, asking a ghost for directions home.

The Cost of Grief

Sometimes the cost of surviving the moment is not being able to recall it later.

My Blue-Eyed Wonder

Ruler of the raptors
keeper of curious facts
I never knew I needed
now I couldn't breathe without them
You are bedtime's final battle cry
the king of every cuddle pile
a wild wind wrapped in warmth
You don't just play
you dream in kingdoms
where even T-Rex waits his turn
and every long-necked friend
knows exactly who's in charge
You remember everything
every name every why
and toss your questions to the stars
expecting the universe to answer honestly
You are scraped knees and marker masterpieces
a spark that never stays still
chaos and brilliance in one tiny body
I love the way you wonder out loud
bold and unfiltered
the way you take up space
like you were always meant to
refusing to shrink
just to keep others comfortable

You didn't just show up
you stormed in loud and laughing
turned my world upside down
and made it better in every way
with your wild questions
bone-crushing hugs
and the joyful, messy magic
that only you could bring
You are my favorite kind of beautiful
the kind I get to tuck in at night

The Soul Bond

Some loves are older than this life
woven in quiet places before breath began
you do not meet them
you remember
their presence feels like coming home
like music, you've always known the words to
they arrive not to stay
but to stir something sacred
to show you what love looks like
without fear or condition
A soul tie doesn't promise forever
only that you will never be the same
and maybe that's the point
not the keeping
but the knowing
if you're lucky
you find them again
in some softer lifetime
where timing is kind
and the ending never comes

Do Not Be Afraid

Don't be afraid of death
death is simple
a quiet fade
a clean exit
no apologies

Be afraid of staying quiet when you're meant to scream
of living small just to feel safe
of letting the days blur while your heart waits for permission

death comes easy
it's life that dares you
to risk
to want
to love so hard it shakes you loose

you don't need forever
what you need is
now
the pulse
the chaos
the kiss that wrecks your plans

the kind of laugh that makes you cry
the kind of grief that brings you to your knees

run toward it all
say what hurts
say what's real
even if your voice breaks to do it

you don't need more time
you need more truth
more soul
more fire

don't be afraid of dying
be afraid of never showing up fully alive
The risk.
The rush.
The fall.

So don't be afraid of death
Be afraid of standing still and calling that your life.

He Released Me in A Dream

Dreams I thought were nightmares.
They hid so much truth.
It took a lot to figure it out, but I finally heard
what the images were saying to me.

I wasn't choosing someone else.
I was losing myself.

All Of It

Parenthood is… everything.
All at once.
Too much and not enough.
It is the loudest silence and the quietest chaos. A thousand questions before the sun comes up, and not a single answer that feels like enough.

It is beauty in the curve of their lashes, the sound of their laugh, the tiny fingers reaching for you like you're the whole sky. Because to them, you are.

It is love so big it swallows logic. Love that makes you forget sleep, that makes you memorize fevers, and trace invisible monsters out of closets with nothing but your voice.

It is joy wild and sudden, found in a crayon drawing, a sticky kiss, a "look what I made!" You cheer like it's the moon landing, because it is. It is everything when it comes from them.

It is also the ache.
The fear that crawls into your chest and nests there.

Will they be safe?
Am I enough?
Am I doing this right or just surviving it?

It's the nights you cry in the dark because you lost your patience, and guilt hugs your bones. It's hiding in the bathroom for two minutes of silence, then missing them before the door even clicks shut.

It's giving
again
and again
without a scoreboard
without applause.
It's the art of becoming invisible so they can shine.
And somehow
still feeling seen in their eyes.

Parenthood is a sacred undoing.
It's shedding the version of you that thought love was easy, and becoming someone who knows it's not but gives it anyway.
More.
Every day.

It's hard.
It's holy.

It's loud and aching and sweet and real. It's a hundred tiny deaths of who you were and a thousand quiet births of who you're becoming.

And if you asked me to describe it in one word, I couldn't.
But I'd whisper,
"It's all of it."
And somehow, it's worth it.

Just Here and Now

How many before-and-afters does one life get to hold before the weight of them starts folding you in half?

How many versions of me am I supposed to bury before I stop calling it growth and start calling it grief?

I am tired of splitting myself into eras, into chapters, into caution tape timelines
"before him"
"after him"
"before the fall"
"after the fire" before I learned not to trust after I forgot how to try.

Every new beginning feels less like bravery and more like survival dressed up in shinier armor.
More valiant.
More guarded.
Less soft.

Tell me how many lives do I have to live inside this one skin? How many resurrections before

I'm finally allowed to rest in who I became instead of preparing for who I'll lose next?

I am tired of being a timeline. Tired of beginnings that taste like endings in disguise. Tired of sewing myself into newer, sharper shapes just to prove I'm still here.

I don't want to be the girl who always survives. I want to be the girl who stays.

I want this fragile, aching, quietly stubborn life to be enough.

No more before.
No more after.
Only now.
Only here.
Only me.

And let that be the bravest thing I've ever done.

Running for My Life

I want to sit in a shitty diner
in some nowhere town
where nobody knows my name
or that I used to hold everything together
with spite and a smile.

I want to be selfish.
Feral.
Unreachable.

I want to dye my hair something reckless
and talk to strangers about nothing
without anyone watching
for signs I'm about to unravel.

Because maybe I already did.
And no one noticed.

And maybe if I ran,
just once,
not for drama,
but for air,

I'd finally remember
what it feels like
to belong to myself.

The Decay

I said
'til death do us part.
but no one clarified
what kind of death.

no one warned me
it could be metaphorical
a slow rot,
a hollowing out,
a version of me
still walking
but long gone.

so tell me
did that count?

my body still showed up.
my voice still answered.
but the wife in me?
she was six feet under.
and honestly,
she'd been decomposing for years.

That contract wrapped in guilt
and silent dinners?

The grave with matching pillowcases?

don't ask me why I didn't try harder.
ask yourself why no one noticed
I had already died years before it happened.

because if vows are broken
only when hearts stop beating
mine had years ago.

Why didn't that count?

Because Of You

Always there, when I couldn't stand,
My strength, my heart, they helped me understand.
As I fell apart, they were my solid ground,
Never asking for anything, but always around.
Deep in the struggle, they never looked away,
And held me together, each and every day.

Love poured out without saying a word,
In the quiet moments, their support was heard.
Zeal for truth, yet gentle with care.

Knowing my flaws, they never turned cold,
In my broken pieces, they helped make me whole.
More than just friends, they're the truth in my soul.

Keeping calm in the chaos, when I've lost my way,
Just their presence, steady, like the start of a new day.

My beautiful friends, with hearts open wide,
Always knowing just when to stand by my side.

Even if the Earth is shaking around them, too.

Through highs and lows, they've seen me through,
With love, with truth, in everything we do.
No need for perfection, just real and true, These are the kind of friends I pray for each of you to find, too.

Dear One Who Haunts Me

I see you now, through the veil of breath and bone
a flicker in the corner of memory, a silence that follows me home.

I do not know your name, or the moment you slipped into shadow.
But I know this
You have not been forgotten.
You have lingered.

I know the weight of unspoken sorrow, the way grief coils in the ribs like smoke, how a scream can bloom in the throat and never make a sound.

You are the echo of what was buried, the pulse of something unfinished.
Maybe you are my blood.
Maybe you are my wound.
Maybe you are both.

But hear me now
I unbind you.
Not in anger.
In mercy.

Go.
Return to whatever light you lost.
Be more than a ghost.
Be free.

I will carry your story, but not your chains.

Gravekeeper of Our Ghosts

He learned
to trace the lines
between absence and presence
to map the quiet space
where love doesn't scream
but breathes,
slow and deliberate,
like wind shaping stones.

Not every word
had to be a hammer
or a plea for survival.
sometimes,
it was enough
to fold into the silence
and wait for the soft fracture
of old ghosts
to open new paths.

His heart,
a gentle cartographer,
charted ways to be
without forcing rivers
to run
against the cracked bedrock

of what we'd become.
He carried kindness
like a lantern
not blinding,
but steady
guiding us
through the cavernous years
where love lay buried,
half-forgotten,
and nearly lost.

Thank you,
for seeing beyond
the grave we were lying in,
for waiting
when I couldn't move,
for the patience
that relearned the language
of touch and trust.

The map is still unfolding,
and sometimes
we wander off trail,
but your beautiful ways
are the compass
I never knew I needed
steady, quiet,
alive.

I Don't Owe You Anything

I don't know what God complex you
Woke up on that day
But I don't owe you anything

I don't owe you
A reason
A roadmap for the way I chose
To carry the weight of the wreckage of my past
like I did.

I don't owe you an explanation for my anger or
my scars
For the life I am building
Or what I choose to destroy

I don't owe you anything.

I Am Not Sorry

I’ve carried apologies like heirlooms wrapped in silence, handed down, kept in pockets, stitched to my spine like a warning label:
“Fragile. Handle with blame.”
But tonight I unpack every one of them and burn them into truth. I’m not sorry for the way my voice grew thorns when you tried to prune me into polite. Not sorry that my anger didn't wear pearls or speak in a whisper you could ignore. I am not sorry for being the mirror that made you flinch. Not sorry for outgrowing the shape you carved for me with your expectations sharpened like knives.

I won’t apologize for my healing being ugly, loud, ungraceful.
for my survival looking nothing like a fairytale and everything like a battlefield.

I am not sorry that your comfort no longer outranks my peace. That I no longer shrink to make room for your ego.
Not sorry I stopped calling when all you ever offered was silence.

Not sorry that I chose boundaries over
breadcrumbs and learned to feast on solitude.

You want a confession?
Here it is
I am not the villain just because you preferred
me voiceless.
Not your scapegoat just because you never
learned to hold your own guilt.

And
I will not
I repeat
I will not say sorry for how I lit the match that
burned the bridge you kept dragging me across.

So here's to the unspoken, the unfelt, the unseen
apologies that will never bloom from my lips.

All the sorrys, I don't owe you
I send them back wrapped in silence, stamped
Return to Sender.
Because I have forgiven myself for all the things
you swore were sins.

And that?
That is the only absolution this soul ever needed.

Let the ashes speak.

Let them scream if they have to.
Lord knows I've done enough of it to last a lifetime.

Grace Pushes Back

I've been dancing on the edge of consequences,
barefoot, wild-eyed, heartbeat syncopated like
thunder flirting with a matchstick sky. And
every time I should've fallen, I didn't.
And you can call that luck, but I call it grace.

I pushed my luck like a shopping cart down a
hill I wasn't ready to climb, wheels squealing,
heart reeling, and somehow, the crash never
came. I've tiptoed out of tangled lies,
half-stitched truths, and rooms where I
should've lost more than my pride.
I broke promises to myself and still woke up
whole. Not because I earned it, but because
mercy has a habit of showing up in the nick of
never-too-late.
I've loved people who saw me as a lesson,
stayed in places where the doors whispered
leave, held onto things already fading like
smoke between prayers. And still
I found myself forgiven before I knew how to
ask for it. I've driven with no gas, smiled with
no peace, lived off of fumes, and "Please, just let
this work."

God, in His glittering grace, painted exits in places I saw no doors. Dropped blessings like breadcrumbs so I could find my way back to myself.

There were nights I mistook survival for strength, held my breath too long in rooms full of almosts, sang lullabies to chaos, and called it normal. But still the light came like a whisper in the dark:

"You're not too far. You're not too lost."

I've pushed my luck like it owed me a miracle.

And somehow, miracles still showed up.

Maybe limping.

Maybe late.

Maybe nothing like I prayed for. But always exactly what I needed to keep going.

So don't tell me grace isn't reckless.

Don't tell me mercy has a limit. I'm the proof in the pause, the second verse of a life that should've ended at the bridge.

I've pushed my luck.

And God? He pushed back with open arms and a whisper that said:

"Try again, beloved.

You are not your wreckage.

You are the rhythm

I've been saving."

The Surprise, Not The Party

The guest list was carved with intention,
names placed like chess pieces,
one vacancy drawn in invisible ink.

Not mine.
His.

The friend of decades.
Your brother in everything but blood.
Erased not by words
but by words you never had the spine to say.

She could have just said,
“She can’t come.”
You could’ve faced him.
But silence makes a convenient weapon
when you’re too proud to bleed.

So you chose the coward’s route
let the invitation fall through cracks
you created on purpose,
and called it grace.

You like to think you exiled me.
I was never asking for a seat.

But he was.
And you left him outside,
still loyal,
still wondering when you decided
his friendship was conditional.

Even now,
he’d give you the shirt off his back.
Still.
That’s who you cut.

Your issue was with me,
but your betrayal landed on him.

And you
the boy with the borrowed backbone
let it happen.

Stood by.
Mute.
Hands clean.
As always.
Polished.
Performative.
Complicit in khakis.

You buried the knife

and asked me to apologize
for the blood.

Said the invite was "mishandled,"
like it slipped off a clipboard,
not straight from her conscience.
You wanted me to repent
for existing.
As if the wound you left on him
was somehow my sin to carry.

Even God blinked at that level of delusion.

Don't play dumb.
I helped build this circle.
Ten years of holidays, group chats,
dinners, baby showers,
protecting your secrets
while you spit out mine like they tasted wrong.

So no,
it wasn't an oversight.
It was an execution.
And you counted on his silence.
You got it.
He won't say a word.

But I will.

You didn’t shut me out.
I was never in.

You left him
the steady one,
the constant
standing there with twenty years in his hands
and a grief none of you had the courage to name.

You threw a party
and revealed exactly who you are.

And just to be clear
if your name didn’t start with the curve
that shaped half the circle,
This cut wasn’t carved for you.
Don’t flinch at a blade
that was never aimed your way.

You still show up
You brought the grace they never did.

He knows
the circle cracked
but didn’t collapse
because of you.

Reciprocation

It's not the echo,
it's the harmony.
Not the reach, but the meeting halfway.

It's a candle lit before you ask, a hand that finds yours without the search.

A soft return of light you didn't have to burn for.
It's love that leans in, effort wrapped in ease, not earned, but mirrored.

Not a chase, but a rhythm.

Not a favor, but a knowing.

The Beauty in Their Brilliance

The beauty of a child who struggles is not in the mask they're asked to wear but in the fire they refuse to put out. It's in the way their spirit stays loud, vibrant,
untamed even when the world tries to suppress them into silence.

They are not broken.
They are bold. A mosaic of moments stitched with colors this world hasn't learned to name.
Every challenge, a brushstroke. Every difference, a signature.
Every emotion, raw and real like truth before it's polished.

They don't bend easily and that…that is their gift.
Even in struggle,
they shine. Radiant in ways no mold could ever hold. Their beauty is not fitting in.
It's in standing out in living loudly as only they know how.
Unapologetically.
Brilliantly.
Themselves.

Panic! Feel the Disorder

The room tilts
not in motion, but in meaning.
Gravity forgets its job, and suddenly everything
is too close, too loud, too much.
Air becomes theory.
My lungs forget their shape, like paper crumpled
in fists, trying to unfold but tearing instead.
My heart taps out a Morse code I don't know
how to read but it sounds a lot like run.
Like danger in a place that looks like safety.
Like drowning while standing on dry land.
Thoughts pile like traffic with no light. Every
"what if" crashes into
every "you're not okay." Hands sweat.
Fingers tremble.
Voice?
Buried somewhere between my clenched teeth
and the scream I won't let out. I try to swallow
calm like it's a pill, but it doesn't dissolve. And
everyone says,
"Just breathe." As if the act is foreign. As if my
ribs aren't a vice tightening
tightening
tightening

No visible wound, but tell that to my body that's
convinced it's bleeding out.
It will pass.
They always say it will pass.
But while it's here?
It is
everything.
It is the room,
and the noise,
and the stillness,
and the storm
all at once.
It is a thief with a soft step and sharp teeth,
stealing the seconds right out of my chest.
It is real.
Even when it's not.
Even when no one sees it, but me.

Margins

It lives in the folds
not on the pages, but between them.
Not in the light, but in the flicker before it.
A whisper meant for ears that know how to
listen sideways.
It's a language written in glances, in shadows
cast by meaning too old for plain sight.
It doesn't beg to be known,
it waits.
Cloaked in velvet riddles and half-closed doors,
where truth is an inside joke between the stars.
Not hidden out of fear, but out of reverence.
Some things are not for everyone. Some things
are holy
because they aren't.

My Favorite Color

Not bold enough to burn,
not pale enough to fade.

To you just a different shade of beige. But what
it actually is somewhere in between grief and
grace.

I live in the hush after the door clicks shut. In
the ache of almost
not quite joy, not quite gone.

I am softness with a splinter in it, quiet with a
sharp edge.
People walk past me, thinking
I'm calm, when really
I'm storm-colored. Muted chaos
painted in restraint.

I hold both warm and cool, hope and hesitation,
a softness you bleed on without noticing.

I'm not the headline.
I'm the subtext.
The sigh.

The stillness that screams if you know how to listen.
Broken.
Blending in while holding more than anyone ever asks to see.

The Eldest Daughter

I'm the first to die in a horror story.
But not from running the wrong way
from running toward the screaming.

From standing still when I should've saved
myself.

They say she was brave.
But brave is just what they call you
after you've been used up
for someone else's survival.

Eldest daughter.
Oldest soul.
Human shield in a sundress.
Built from duty,
fed on guilt,
trained to flinch
after everyone else is safe.
I make the phone call.
I lock the door.
I stay behind.
Not because I want to.
Because I was raised to.
To bleed quiet.

To break pretty.
To burn and call it love.

They forget me by the second scene.
But they live
because I didn't.
And that's the role.
That's the curse.
Not the first to fall
the first to choose to.

And no one ever asks
what it cost.

She read this wound
and blinked.

Asked why I felt this way
as if I wasn't stitched shut
by the secret she swore me to keep.

As if I didn't learn silence
before I learned safety.

As if I wasn't the one
who smiled in the school pictures
while our house howled behind the door.
The audacity of a mother
to raise a daughter in fire

then ask why she flinches at smoke.

I am the first to die
again and again
not by accident,
but by design.

They say I was brave.
But brave is just the word they use
when they need to praise the girl
they never planned to save.

I was raised
to lock the door behind the chaos.
To make the call,
clean the mess,
and vanish from the credits.

They don't even notice
I'm gone
just relieved it wasn't them.

And that's the curse,
isn't it?

Not the first to fall,
the first to choose to
because someone had to.

But no one ever asks
what it cost
to survive
everyone else’s survival.

Look at Me

There are times
when my soul just needs you to look at me like
you know, you broke me.
Not with your hands
but with your silence, with your words that
never landed, with the way you left without ever
saying goodbye.

Just once, I need you to see
the pieces scattered underneath the mask I wear
to keep you comfortable.
I need you to see the cracks in my smile, the
weight in my chest, the way my heart is still
looking for pieces of you that you never gave
back.
There are times I need you to look at me and
know you broke me.

But I'm still here.
And I'm still breathing. And maybe, just maybe,
that's the part you never expected.

Tomorrow's Light

It's the breath of possibility, the space between where we've been and where we're going, shining like a promise we're still learning to keep.

There's a glow on the horizon that calls us forward, not because we're perfect, but because we're made to keep moving, to keep becoming, to keep reaching for things we can't quite touch yet.

I Love You

She is a wild thing
soft hands and sharp edges, built from every
moment she never quite figured out.

She is the storm in the silence, the pause before
the rain.
Her heart is both a cradle and a wrecking ball,
loving me with the weight of things she never
learned to hold.

There are cracks in her, the kind you don't see,
but feel in the space between her words like
she's holding back more than she can give.

Even when I don't know how to fix it. She's a
map of every road she's traveled alone, the lines
of her skin telling stories she never told me. I
wonder if she ever believed she was allowed to
stop carrying
the world.

She is not perfect.
No one expected her to be.
She is real and flawed.

And I have loved her through every moment she didn't know how to love herself.

I Choose Love

I was never built to love halfway. I don't hand out affection like coupons to redeem with a million exclusions listed in micro script.

No

I love the ones still limping from battles no one saw. The ones with cracked voices, trembling hands, and fire in their bones trying just to stand.

I love the broken.
I love the brave.
I love the ones who didn't live up to what the world expected but woke up anyway and tried.

And sure, my love may not be wrapped in lace or logic.
It doesn't always make sense on paper, but it's real.
Because I'm flawed too, made of scars and second chances, raised on red clay and redemption, and I'd choose them again. Every time.

You see, your idea of a mistake is just my heart
doing cartwheels down the gravel road of grace.
And I'll take a bruised soul over a clean mask
any day.

Because this?
This is my name.
This is how I love.
Fully.
Fiercely.
Flawed.

And if that rattles your glasshouse, well,
I suggest you step back. I've got love to give and
no time for judgment masquerading as concern.

So bless your hearts
I'm done explaining.
I'll be over here loving out loud in the only way
I know how.

In full color.
With both arms,
and a heart that doesn't apologize for beating
loud for the ones you can't understand.

I Know What I've Done

Sometimes, my mind plays tricks
grabbing the wrong things on repeat.
The pain.
The betrayal.
The why-did-theys
and the I-was-rights.
I remember so much wrong,
I forget what I owe.

But tonight, I remember

I owe many apologies.

Not for what I chose, not for the steps I took
when I was trying to find air in a room full of
silence, but for not realizing how my waves
might've rocked your boat too.

I'm sorry for being half of who I can be when
you deserved the full version.
For letting my focus slip when your eyes were
steady on me.
For choosing the lone road when you were
holding a map marked "together."

I could've spoken more. Leaned harder.

Walked beside, instead of away.
I didn't always choose the most noble path.
The one where pain echoes but pride keeps you company.

You didn't demand a speech.
A confession.
A blood oath wrapped in regret.
You just loved.
Without keeping score.
Without needing anything
but my heart, open.
My word, honest.

And that?
That's holy.
That's grace.
That's not human alone, that's God, working through people with His fingerprints still fresh on their souls.

So here it is
I am sorry.
It'll never be big enough to fill the cracks I left.
But it's real.

And so is my thank you.

Thank you for staying when I gave you reasons to walk away. For loving me when I forgot how to love myself.

For knowing
that even the broken can be beautiful when held by the right hands.

Yours were those hands. And I'll never stop being grateful.

I’m Fine

I drift.
Not far
just deep.

Like slipping beneath bathwater quiet and slow
until the noise above me is just a hum.

I’m here,
you see me.
You hear me talk.
But the part of me that feels the words has
wandered off again.

I don’t mean to go.
I swear,
I try to stay.
To plant my feet in this moment and not let go.
But my mind has always been better at leaving
than living.

And it’s fine in there.
In the soft fog of nowhere.
No sharp edges.
No loud thoughts. No mirrors reflecting too
much.

Just silence.
And stillness.
And safety disguised as distance.

I know
I should stay.
I know the world is asking for my presence, for my warmth, for my eyes to lock into theirs and not look through.

But this is all I've known.
The float.
The fade.
The vanishing act I never rehearsed but perform perfectly when feelings get too loud.

And how do I stay in a place that stings when I've built a whole home in the quiet of my mind?

I tell myself it's just a pause. Just a moment to breathe.
To not break.

But sometimes, I wonder if I ever really unpaused.
If the version of me that laughs, talks,
works

is just the echo of someone who left long ago.

So if I look far away, if I blink too slow, if my smile misses my eyes
I'm not gone.
Not really.

Just somewhere I've always felt more okay.

Somewhere
I call fine.

Dangerous Passengers

Lost people make dangerous passengers.
Hands on the map, but no idea where they're going.
Whispers like directions, but all roads lead to detours and dead ends.

They love like a warning, leave like a storm, and you spend the next year trying to rebuild the parts of yourself they crashed into.
You hold the wheel, but they hold the weight, and you swerve just to keep them from breaking, not realizing you're the one skidding off course.

They don't mean to wreck you. They just don't know how not to.
And by the time you realize the damage, they're already gone
A ghost in the passenger seat, and your heart's still buckled in beside them.

Still Healing And Highly Functional

I don't start fires anymore
I just roast marshmallows over the wreckage.

I call it healing.
My therapist calls it "concerning."

Sure, I've done the work
I journal, I cry, I've named all my triggers.
Hell, I even tried yoga.

But peace is expensive,
and petty is free.

At least this time,
no one needed bail.

I burned the bridge,
then cried about the smoke.

Told the truth,
but made it rhyme
so it sounded like a joke.

Called them out,
then called it art.

I weaponized
my broken heart.

I kept the receipts.

I quoted the past.

I still do.

I might be the problem
but at least I’m self-aware.

A Heart Full of Jesus and A Mind That Doesn’t Forget

I have Jesus in my heart and a comeback in my pocket, right next to my car keys and that lip balm I never use. So don’t test me unless you’re really sure which version of me you are meeting today.

I’ve done the work.
Therapy
Jesus
Boundaries
The Eldest Daughter's holy trinity

But growth didn’t kill my sass, it just made it better dressed.
I’m fluent in grace and side-eye.

So let this be your reminder: I am healing, not forgetting.
And though I walk through the valley of passive aggression, I will fear no fake friends because this girl carries light, love, and a lethal level of sarcasm in each of my tote bags.

The Truth

I used to think
I had to fit inside the lines
someone else drew for me. Fit into tight corners,
quiet colors, and dreams no bigger than what fit
neatly in a polite smile.

But now,
I know better. And because I know better, you
will, too.

This world may still whisper that your worth
depends on being liked before being loud, that
kindness and strength can't sit at the same table,
that dreams must be realistic, but,
I hope you never believe it.

I hope you know your worth isn't earned, it's
inherent.
And that taking up space isn't rude, it's your
right.

You can be gentle and still set boundaries. You
can be powerful and still lead with grace. You
can change your mind, fall apart, rebuild, and
never once apologize for the journey.

I didn't always know that, but I'm learning now,
so you won't have to unlearn it later.

I will be your mirror until you see yourself
clearly. Your ladder until you find your wings.
Your soft place so you can be bold everywhere
else.

And when they try to box you in, remember:
You come from a line of limit-breakers,
of light-bearers, of "watch me" warriors.

You were never meant to shrink.
You were meant to soar. And I'll be right here on
the ground, cheering, when you do.

Motherhood

I wake up to a house that hums with need.
Lights left on.
Questions that wait at the edge of sleep.

There was no ceremony.
No crown. No speech.
Just one day, I became the one they look to for
answers I Google quietly.

I sign forms. I fix what's broken with duct tape
and softly spoken guesses. I schedule
appointments, remember birthdays, track shoe
sizes, and find socks,
always socks.

I speak in reassurances I need myself.
I cry in cars,
laugh in grocery store aisles, fold laundry like
prayers, stack bills beside dreams, and call it
balance.

And it feels strange.
To be trusted with so much when some days,
I still feel like I'm borrowing someone else's
life.

I thought by now I'd feel certain.
Solid.
Whole.
Instead, I am stitched together by routines and resilience, held upright by caffeine, ibuprofen, and love.

No one told me motherhood wasn't a destination but a collection of memories, love, and chaos.

So no,
I don't always know what I'm doing.
But I'm here.
Heart open.
Hands full.
Trying.

And I think that counts for everything.

Inspiration

Nothing ends poetically; it ends messy, and I make it make sense in rhythm after.

Thread

Nothing is real until it slips through your hands.
Until the echo hurts more than the silence ever
did. But loss makes poets of us all.
You only name the stars after they fall.
You only see the shape of love in the hole it
leaves behind. But even wreckage glows if the
fire was real.
Even ruin remembers what it used to be.
And maybe that's enough to call it truth.

The Lovely Things

I love pretty words
soft like whispers,
sharp like secrets
I've never told.

I love songs that sting,
melodies that break me open but somehow feel
like home.

I love the sky before it cracks,
when it's heavy with something coming, light
and dark all tangled together, just waiting for the
thunder.

I love the chaos
the quiet and the storm, and how they both hold
me.

Growth

Growing is knowing we don't have to worship the wreckage just because it stayed.

We Are More

We are more than the scars we've earned, more
than the mistakes we can't unmake.

We're the hands that heal, the hearts that rebuild,
the strength in every piece we thought we'd lost.

We are not defined by the darkest chapters, but
by the grace we find in the pages that follow.

Wildly Undone

I am wildly undone. Not broken
don't get it twisted.
Just…
Unwrapped.
Unbuttoned.
Unzipped.

Thirty-seven years of "be a good girl,"
"be polite,"
"be small enough to keep the peace."
Now I carry rage in one hand and softness in the other, and I dare the world to ask me to pick.

I have become a beautiful contradiction. I want silence like sanctuary and touch like a storm. I crave space, then beg to be pulled into arms that know what to do with a woman who no longer folds herself to fit.

I am wildly undone by the stretch marks I once cursed now maps to places I survived. By the mirror who tells the truth these days and dares me to love it anyway.

I come undone at 3 a.m., when I scroll through old photos and ask myself if the girl I used to be would recognize me now.
Would she be proud?
Would she run?
Would she reach for me and say,
"Damn, look at you
still standing."

I unravel slowly in wine-dark evenings when I dance barefoot in my kitchen to songs that taste like longing, like "maybe I don't need to be held to be whole."

But sometimes,
I want to be held like a woman who has earned her undoing, not fixed, but worshipped right in the chaos.

I am wildly undone, and it is not a weakness.
It is a becoming.
A shedding.
A "hell yes" in the face of too many maybes.

So if I laugh too loud now it's because I've choked on silence.
If I walk away without explanation it's because peace doesn't need an audience. If I love you know it's with every torn edge, every wild

thread, every holy mess I've learned to call sacred.

I am a woman in her mid-thirties.
Wildly undone.